Rays

Rays

A Carolrhoda Nature Watch Book

by Sally M. Walker

Carolrhoda Books, Inc. / Minneapolis

For the staff members at the North Carolina Aquarium-Fort Fisher. For more than 10 years of North Carolina vacations, they patiently answered my family's questions about our beachcombing treasures. The ray tank provided hours of entertainment, too.

The author wishes to thank Dr. Roger Klocek, Dr. Carl Luer, Dr. Leonard Compagno, and Michael Janech for answering her many questions about rays. Dr. Compagno also provided invaluable assistance with the chart on pages 44 and 45.

Text copyright © 2003 by Sally M. Walker

Carolrhoda Books, Inc.
A division of Lerner Publishing Group
241 First Avenue North
Minneapolis, MN 55401 U.S.A.

Website address: www.lernerbooks.com

Library of Congress Cataloging-in-Publication Data

Walker, Sally M.
    Rays / by Sally M. Walker.
      p.   cm. — (A Carolrhoda Nature Watch Book)
    Summary: Describes the physical characteristics, behavior, life cycle, and endangered status of rays.
    ISBN: 1–57505–172–9 (lib. bdg. : alk. paper)
    1. Rays (Fishes)—Juvenile literature. [1. Rays (Fishes)
2. Endangered species.] I. Title. II. Nature watch
(Minneapolis, Minn.)
QL638.8 .W25 2003
597.3'5—dc21   2001006586

Manufactured in the United States of America
1 2 3 4 5 6 – JR – 08 07 06 05 04 03

CONTENTS

A Fascinating Flat Fish   6
Physical Characteristics   13
Hunting and Eating   20
A Ray's World   23
Stings and Shocks   31
Life Cycle   34
Rays and People   41
Glossary   46
Index   47

A FASCINATING FLAT FISH

A small fish slowly swims along the quiet, sandy ocean floor. It nibbles on a piece of drifting seaweed. Suddenly, the sandy bottom seems to explode. A flat fish darts up from the sand. Its strong, winglike fins push it up and over the small fish. The flat fish quickly gobbles up the smaller fish and then settles back to the ocean floor. Within seconds, the flat fish covers itself with sand again and becomes almost invisible.

This flat fish is called a ray. Mostly, rays hide motionless on a sandy ocean or river bottom. But when they swim, they become graceful underwater "flyers."

Because most rays live along the bottoms of oceans and some rivers, people have always had trouble learning much about them. For centuries, many humans feared rays, believing they were monsters with strange powers.

The ancient Greeks and Romans told stories of one kind of ray with a dangerous **spine.** A Roman writer named Pliny the Elder reported that some rays had tail spines sharp enough to pierce metal armor. Indeed, ray spines have been widely used as weapons—most often on spears—by people in places from Greece to Central America to Australia. Ancient people knew that most ray spines were poisonous, which made them even more dangerous. Pliny wrote that the poison was strong enough to kill trees. To make matters worse, people believed rays could shoot their spines, like arrows, at ocean bathers and seaside wanderers. No wonder people feared rays!

Since then, people have learned more about rays. They are not fearsome monsters. Unless disturbed, they are peaceful creatures. And rays are fascinating: their bodies have undergone remarkable changes so that they are able to live near the ocean floor or on a river bottom.

Opposite page: *These rays have sharp spines on their tails. Rays' spines were once used by humans as weapons.*
Above: *Most rays live near the bottom of the ocean.*

7

Scientists classify, or sort, animals into groups according to characteristics they share. Rays, sharks, and several other types of fishes belong to a class, or large grouping, of fishes called Chondrichthyes (kahn-DRIHK-theez). Fishes in the class Chondrichthyes do not have skeletons made of bone, like ours. Instead, their skeletons are made of a softer material called **cartilage.** The tips of your ears and nose are made of cartilage. Cartilage weighs less than bone. The lighter weight makes swimming easier.

Along with rays, the class Chondrichthyes includes such fishes as the spotted ratfish (top) *and the whitetip reef shark* (bottom). *All these fishes have skeletons of cartilage instead of bone.*

Scientists believe rays evolved from sharks. Over millions of years, some sharks **adapted,** or changed. They adapted to living on or near the bottom of oceans and rivers, where it was easier to find and catch food. Their teeth became flat instead of sharp, which was better for crushing shellfish found on the bottom. Their rounded, sharklike bodies became flattened, so they could hide in the sand. Their front fins, called **pectoral fins,** got much larger and stronger, and their tails became much smaller. Their pectoral fins also became connected to the sides of their heads.

Rays use their pectoral fins to swim and steer. They also can use their pectoral fins to glide or float in the water or rest on the bottom. **Fossils,** or hardened remains, of ancient rays show that the first true rays lived about 150 million years ago. Compare that to sharks, which have been on the earth for 400 million years.

Ray fossils, like this one, are rare because soft cartilage usually decays and disappears quickly.

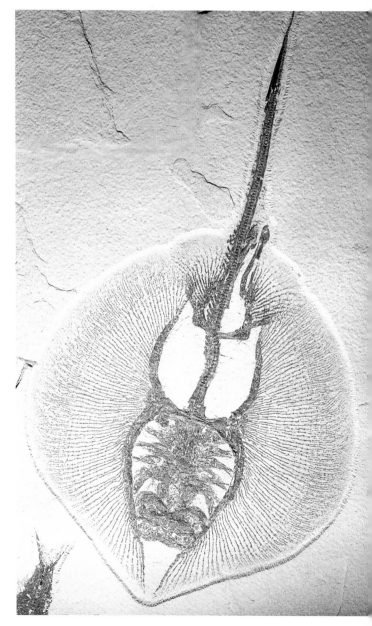

Like most fish, this yelloweye rockfish (below) *has its gill slits on the sides of its body. A ray* (right) *is easy to recognize because its gill slits are on the underside of its body.*

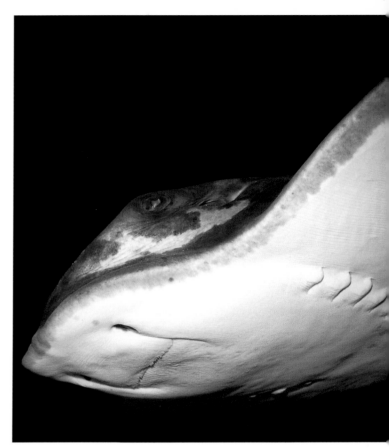

Within the class Chondrichthyes, rays belong to an order, or a slightly smaller group of fishes, known as Rajiformes. Most rays are easily recognized by their flat, disk-shaped bodies and thin tails. But the surest way to recognize a ray is to look for its gill slits, special openings used for breathing. Rays are the only fish whose gill slits are always located on the undersides of their bodies.

Because there are many different kinds of rays, scientists further divide the order Rajiformes into suborders. Among other physical characteristics, the shapes and sizes of the teeth, fins, and snouts help scientists classify rays into particular suborders. Each suborder of rays is broken into even smaller groups called **species.** Animals within a species are able to mate with each other and produce young like themselves.

The largest suborder of Rajiformes contains the rays known as skates. Skates are the only rays that lay eggs. There are more than 230 species of skates.

Stingrays are the second largest suborder of rays. Most stingrays have one or more sharp spines, or stingers, on their tail. The spines are poisonous and can cause a painful wound. Giant manta rays are stingrays. But the manta ray's spine is very small, and some are not poisonous. There are more than 170 species of stingrays.

Electric rays make up the third largest suborder of rays. These rays have special electric organs that can give other animals a powerful electric shock. This comes in handy for defense or when catching **prey,** the animals rays kill and eat. There are about 50 species of electric rays.

Top: *A deepwater skate*
Bottom: *The bluespotted ribbontail ray is a stingray.*

The shark ray is often mistaken for a shark.

The remaining suborders include rays that are often confused with sharks. Their bodies are more rounded than the bodies of other rays, and they have muscular, sharklike tails. But their gill slits are on the underside of their bodies, and that classifies them as rays. A shark's gill slits are along the sides of its body.

These smaller suborders include fishes called guitarfishes, thornback rays, sawfishes, shark rays, panrays, and wedge-fishes. A guitarfish has a flattened, raylike head and a long, sharklike tail, so it looks like a guitar. A wedgefish looks very much like a guitarfish. But there are some important differences in fins and other body structures, so scientists classify wedgefishes separately from guitarfishes. There are only five named species of wedgefishes. The seven species of sawfishes are easily recognized by their long, flat, toothed saws, which stick out from the fish's snout.

PHYSICAL CHARACTERISTICS

Since there are so many species of rays, it isn't surprising that they can be found in a wide range of sizes. Scientists use two measurements to describe the size of a ray. One measurement is the length from the tip of a ray's snout to the tip of its tail. The second measurement describes the size of a ray's **disk,** or the flattened part of its body. This measurement, called the disk width, is the width of the disk from the tip of one pectoral fin to the tip of the other when the fins are spread out.

Some species of round stingrays are only 2 feet (0.6 meter) long and 1 foot (0.3 m) wide. Common stingrays grow to 8 feet (over 2 m) long, with a disk width of up to 4.5 feet (1.4 m). The largest rays are manta rays, which may be more than 22 feet (6.7 m) wide.

Manta rays are the largest rays. The fins on either side of the manta ray's large mouth look like horns. (That's where its nickname, "devil ray," comes from.)

The shape of a ray's disk depends on its species. Electric rays have round disks. Some skates have sharply pointed snouts, which makes their disks diamond shaped. Stingrays can have round or diamond shaped disks. Manta and eagle ray disks look like kites.

The ray's head is part of the disk. Its snout is at the front part of the disk. The mouth is usually on the underside, although a manta's mouth is on the front. A ray's eyes are on the top of the disk.

The ray's pectoral fins make up most of the disk. All rays have large pectoral fins. Muscles in the pectoral fins provide power for swimming. Pectoral fins are also used for steering and making turns.

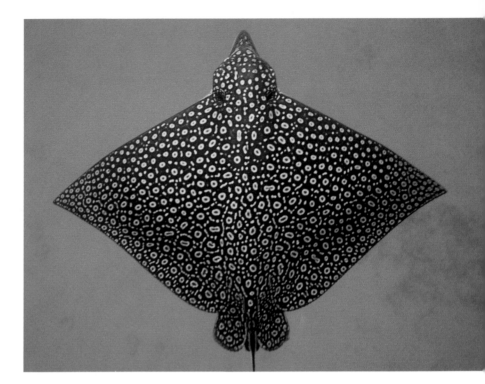

Top: *The spotted eagle ray has a kite-shaped disk.*
Bottom: *This thornback ray shows the underside of its round disk. The mouth and gill slits are visible.*

Smaller fins help keep a ray's body stable while swimming. All rays have two pelvic fins that are located toward the ray's tail. Some rays also have one or two dorsal fins. A ray's dorsal fins are found on the top side of its tail, not on its disk. If a ray has a tail fin, it is toward the tip of its tail.

All rays have tails. Electric rays, sawfishes, and guitarfishes have strong, thick tails used for swimming forward. Skates and stingrays have less powerful tails. They rely on their pectoral fins for most of their forward motion. A skate's tail is fairly short. A stingray's tail is long and thin, almost like a whip.

Male rays have two **claspers** near their pelvic fins. Claspers are used during mating. Female rays do not have claspers.

You can see this male biscuit skate's claspers next to its tail.

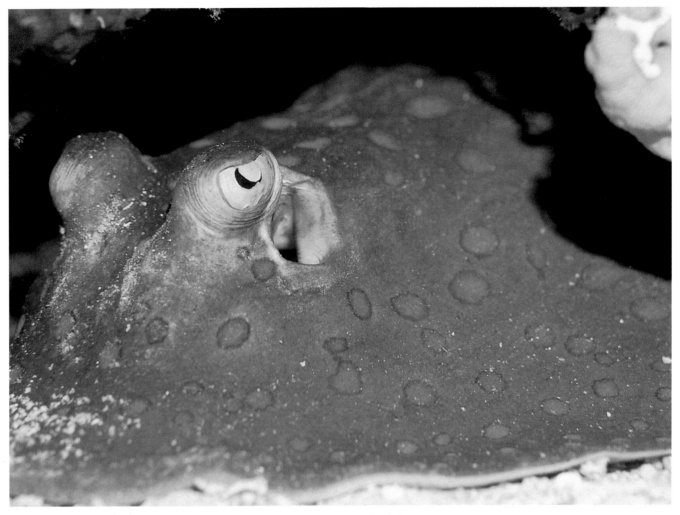

Some rays, such as this bluespotted ribbontail ray, are very colorful.

Rays are usually muted shades of olive green, brown, tan, dark blue, gray, or black. A ray's underside is often a lighter color than its back. A ray may be spotted or striped, or have a lacy pattern of lines. Some spots and lines are bright colors. The bluespotted ribbontail has brilliant blue spots and a blue band on each side of its tail.

Rays have hard, toothlike scales called **denticles** that stick up from their skin. The denticles help protect their bodies from injury. Like some teeth, denticles wear out. When a denticle is too old, it falls out. The denticles that were on either side of the lost denticle grow into the space left behind. Denticles are continually being shed and replaced.

16

Some rays have enlarged denticles, which may appear at the tips of the ray's pectoral fins, along its snout, or along its tail. The enlarged denticles, called **thorns,** may be 2 to 3 inches (5 to 8 centimeters) long. Thorns are not poisonous. The broad skate has a continuous row of 24 to 29 thorns on its back. A row of smaller thorns appears on each side of the central row on the broad skate's tail. Guitarfishes have one line of thorns.

A sawfish probably has the strangest-looking denticles of all. Each of the "teeth" along the sides of a sawfish's saw is an enlarged denticle! Some grow to be 5 inches (13 cm) long. The whole saw may be up to 1 foot (0.3 m) wide and 6 feet (2 m) long.

Left: *The sawfish uses its thorny saw for defense and for hunting.* Below: *The thornback ray has rows of thorns along its back and down its tail.*

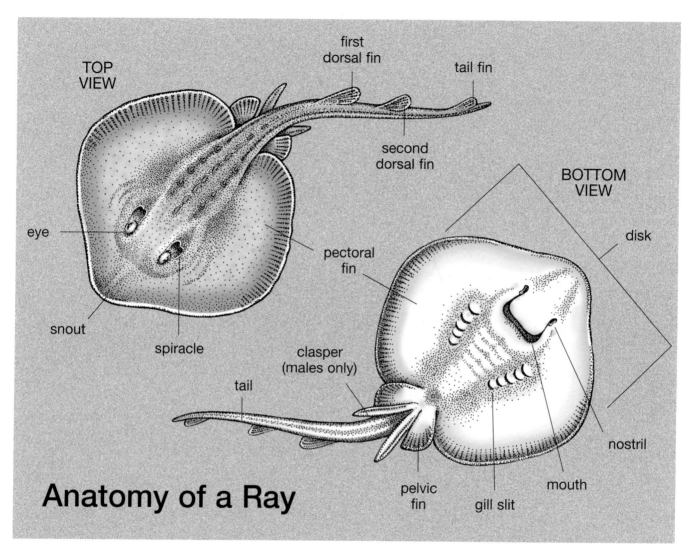

TOP
VIEW

first
dorsal fin

tail fin

second
dorsal fin

BOTTOM
VIEW

eye

disk

pectoral
fin

snout

spiracle

clasper
(males only)

nostril

tail

mouth

pelvic
fin

gill slit

Anatomy of a Ray

Most fishes have gill slits on the sides of their heads. But rays have their gill slits on the underside of their disks. The gill slits lead to the ray's **gills.** Rays need to breathe oxygen to live, and they use their gills to get oxygen from the water. A ray pulls water into its body through its gill slits, and the water passes over its gills. Blood vessels in the gills remove oxygen from the water and carry it to other parts of the ray's body.

Most rays spend most of their time on the bottoms of oceans and rivers. If a ray lying on the bottom tried to pull water in through its gill slits, sand would be sucked in, too. It could hurt or clog the ray's gills. The ray might suffocate.

Instead, a ray lying on the bottom can pull water into its body through two special holes called **spiracles.** Spiracles are located just behind the eyes. In fact, a ray's spiracles might fool you. When they open and close, they look like blinking eyes.

Valves, or flaps, inside the spiracles allow water to flow in but keep it from flowing out. The water then flows into and over the gills. After the oxygen has been removed, the water passes out of the ray's body through its gill slits. While a ray is buried in sand, it may not be possible for water to go out through its gill slits. In that case, the ray can force water back out through its spiracles. Sometimes sand accidentally falls into a ray's spiracle. When it does, the ray spouts the water and sand back out through the spiracle.

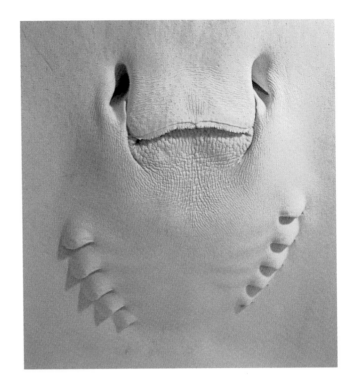

If a ray's gill slits (top) *are buried in the sand, the ray can use its spiracles* (bottom) *to breathe water in and out without also breathing in the sand.*

This southern stingray is hiding in the sand so it can surprise its prey.

HUNTING AND EATING

Rays are **carnivores,** or meat eaters. Depending on the species, rays eat worms, fish, squid, shrimp, crabs, and lobsters. Some eat clams, mussels, oysters, and snails. A ray eats an average of 1 to 2.5 percent of its body weight per day.

Many species of rays spend a large part of their time simply resting, waiting for prey. A ray's color helps it blend in with the bottom. After a ray settles to the bottom, it uses its pectoral fins to dig its way into the sand or mud. Some rays have a slimy substance called mucus on their skin. The mucus coating keeps the sand or mud in place when it settles. When partially covered with sand, a ray is almost impossible to spot. When unsuspecting prey swims close, the ray shoots up and gobbles it down.

Some rays take a more active role in finding and capturing prey. Bat stingrays flap their pectoral fins as they swim along the bottom. The fanning motion sweeps small creatures up into the water. Then the bat stingray swallows them.

A sawfish sifts through the sand with its long saw. The saw stirs up small creatures that live in the sand. A sawfish also swims into schools of small fish. It flails its head from side to side and bashes the fish with its saw. Then it swallows fish that have been stunned by the blows.

Manta rays eat only plankton, tiny organisms that float in the water. The soft flaps of curled skin on either side of the manta ray's large mouth are called cephalic fins. When a manta ray eats, it cruises through the water, mouth opened wide. Its cephalic fins uncurl and scoop plankton and tiny fish into the manta ray's mouth.

Manta rays feeding on plankton at night. The uncurled cephalic fins wave toward the ray's mouth.

Shellfish such as these mussels are easy for a ray to pick out of the sand, but the ray must use its hard teeth and powerful jaws to crush the shells and get to the meat inside.

Each species of ray has the kind of teeth best suited for the kind of food it eats. Barndoor skates and winter skates have sharply pointed teeth, useful for grabbing and holding worms and wiggly fish. Eagle rays have flat teeth good for crushing and grinding the shells of crabs, clams, and snails.

The teeth in a ray's mouth actually evolved from skin denticles. Over millions of years, the denticles near a ray's mouth changed. They developed into rows of teeth. Unlike people, rays have many rows of teeth. Teeth in the first row, near a ray's lips, continually wear out and are replaced. When a tooth falls out, the tooth from the row behind moves forward into the space.

A RAY'S WORLD

A dolphin's graceful leaps and a shark's triangular fin are easily spotted. But most rays are bottom dwellers. Bottom dwellers live on ocean, lake, and river floors. They are not easily seen from a boat—even one set up with video cameras. As a result, rays have not been studied as much in the wild as some other marine creatures have. It is also hard to learn about rays' **habitat.** A habitat is the place where something naturally lives.

Scientists do know that a ray's flat body is perfect for swimming near or hiding on sandy or muddy bottom surfaces. The ray's pectoral fins barely ripple when the ray glides across the bottom. Scientists also know that some rays don't stay on the bottom. Cownose rays, eagle rays, and manta rays swim closer to the surface. When these rays swim, their fins do more than ripple. They flap up and down, as if the rays are flying underwater.

A coffin ray hunts in its habitat.

Since manta rays do not stay on the bottom of the ocean, they are easier to study.

Rays live in all of the earth's seas and in nearby bays and river mouths. Some live in freshwater lakes. Rays can live in many different water temperatures. Some rays, such as manta rays, live only in warm ocean waters. Several species of skates live in the icy Bering Sea and the Gulf of Alaska. Some rays can live in either warm or cold water. The big skate can be found as far north as northwestern Alaska and as far south as southern California.

Most rays are marine fishes, which means they live only in saltwater. For example, skates live only in marine waters. But some rays stray into freshwater. Sawfishes often swim into rivers. They have been found in the lower Mississippi and Amazon Rivers. Several species of marine stingrays can remain for days in freshwater. But then they must return to saltwater.

There are a few species of stingrays that make their home only in freshwater. River stingrays can be found in most of the large rivers in Central and South America. Other freshwater rays live in some rivers and lakes in east Asia and some parts of Africa. Some sawfishes live in Lake Nicaragua, in Central America. Rays may live in shallow or deep water, depending on the species.

Wherever a ray's home might be, it uses its excellent senses to survive there. For example, although rays are often hidden by sand or mud, they still must keep a sharp lookout for **predators,** or animals that would eat them. Because a ray's eyes are on the top surface of its disk, a ray can still look around, even when pressed tightly against the bottom. Each eye has only one moving eyelid—the lower one. The upper eyelid is joined together with the eyeball. Most rays have large, well-developed eyes. But some rays, such as blind torpedos, live in very deep, dimly lit water. Their eyes are tiny.

Top: *The Atlantic stingray can live in either freshwater or saltwater.*
Bottom: *The eye of a winter skate hiding in the sand. Winter skates live at the bottom of the ocean.*

25

A ray uses the two nostrils on the front of its snout to smell the surrounding water and sense nearby prey. Although rays don't have ears on their bodies, they can hear. Ear bones inside a ray's head sense sound vibrations.

In addition to sight, smell, and hearing, rays have two special senses. These senses give them information about their surroundings—especially about the other living creatures around them.

All living creatures produce electrical pulses inside their bodies. The tiny electrical pulses come from muscle activity and chemical reactions that occur in an animal's body. These pulses form weak electric fields. One of a ray's special senses allows it to detect these electric fields.

This New Zealand eagle ray uses its excellent senses to survive in its habitat.

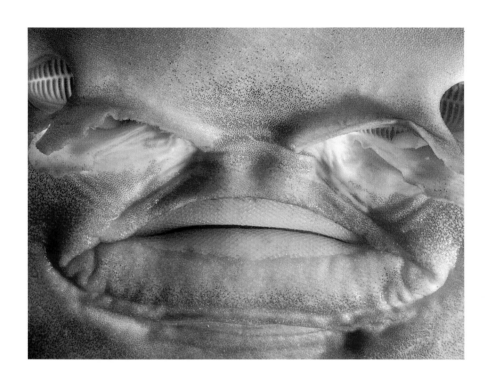

Many tiny pores, or holes, dot the front and underside portion of a ray's body, especially around its mouth. Each pore is the opening of a tiny, jelly-filled tube. Each tube leads to a sac, or pouchlike organ, filled with jelly. These tiny sacs are called **ampullae of Lorenzini** (AM-pyoo-lee of lo-ren-ZEE-nee). Nerves inside the ampullae detect weak electric fields. After a ray senses the prey's electric field, it can zero in for the catch. The ampullae can even sense prey buried in sand or mud. Experiments using captive rays have shown that rays sense buried prey faster by using their ampullae of Lorenzini than they can with their noses. Ampullae of Lorenzini are effective only for detecting prey up to several inches (20–30 cm) away.

A ray's other special sense helps it detect movement in the water. Rays, like many other fishes, have a sensory system called the **lateral line.** The lateral line is a system of canals just below the skin. Lateral line canals are found on a ray's back and underside. They are filled with fluid. Tiny hair cells stick out into the canals. Any animal movement disturbs and moves the surrounding water. When an animal that is close to a ray moves, water flows through pores along the ray's lateral line and moves the hair cells. That lets the ray know a moving object, or possible prey, is nearby.

Clams and other shellfish are typical prey for some rays. These creatures bury themselves in the sand. To breathe, they stick their syphons, or breathing tubes, out from their shells. From time to time, the syphon squirts out a jet of water. Experiments on captive rays have shown that a ray's lateral line, especially the part on the ray's underside, can detect a syphon's water jet. As soon as the lateral line senses the movement, the ray knows right where to go.

When a buried clam squirts water out through its syphon (top), *a ray* (bottom) *detects it with its lateral line and knows just where to go to find a meal.*

28

Cownose rays sometimes migrate in schools of up to 10,000.

Even though it is hard to study rays, scientists are discovering many interesting facts about how rays behave and whether they live alone or in groups. Porcupine river stingrays live alone. They come together only to mate. Manta rays usually swim together in pairs or small groups. Eagle rays have been spotted in large groups of several thousand, called schools, in the waters along the southern California coast.

Many rays **migrate,** or swim to different areas when the seasons or water temperatures change. Some rays like to stay in water that is the same temperature. Some follow their source of food as it migrates. And some may be moving to waters better suited for the survival of baby rays. How far rays migrate depends on the species. Each summer, schools of bluntnose stingrays migrate many miles northward along the Atlantic coast of the United States. Roundrays in California migrate only about 4 to 5 miles (6–8 km).

A ray's special senses are helpful in migration. Scientists think rays may use their ampullae of Lorenzini to sense the earth's magnetic field. The earth's magnetic field causes electric fields in water currents. Using its ampullae, a ray may be able to sense the direction of the flowing electric field. Sensing the direction of an electric field as it moves in water currents may keep rays on track during migration. It's kind of like having their own internal compass.

Schooling eagle rays

Stingrays, such as this bluespotted ribbontail ray, defend themselves with their venomous spines.

STINGS AND SHOCKS

A motionless ray on the bottom looks harmless. And when left alone, it usually is. But some rays have self-defense systems that are very dangerous. They can seriously wound, or even kill, an attacker. The biggest enemies of rays are sharks and humans.

Stingrays are well-known for the painful wounds caused by their spines, sometimes called stingers. Spines are actually denticles that have grown very large, some up to 15 inches (38 cm) long.

Spines are found on the stingray's back near the base of its tail. Most stingrays have one spine, but some species have three or more, one behind the other. The spines on a stingray's tail are venomous—they contain poison. Predators or prey can get stabbed when a stingray whips its tail. When a spine stabs into a victim, venom enters into the wound. If a shark or other creature tries to chomp on a stingray, it may get a big surprise.

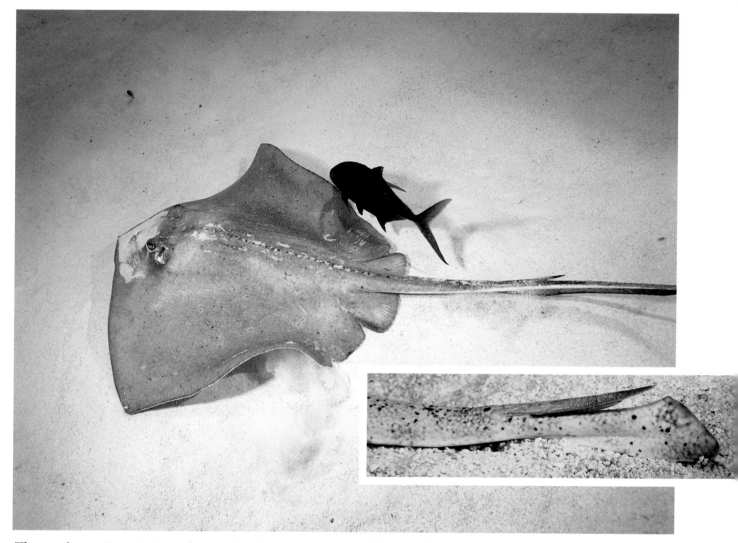

The southern stingray's jagged spine (inset) *can cause a painful wound.*

Stingrays usually leave people alone. And they do not shoot their spines. The reason most people get stabbed by a stingray's spine is because they step on the ray. When a stingray is stepped on, it swings its tail upward. The sharp spine digs into whatever soft body part it hits.

Stingray wounds don't usually kill people. But they are very painful and may take months to heal. When walking in the ocean, it's wise to do the "stingray shuffle." Slide your feet along the sand, instead of lifting them up and down. That way your feet will slide under, rather than land on top of, a partially buried stingray.

Electric rays have special organs that create electricity. There is one organ on each side of an electric ray's disk, near its head. On the outside, the organs are kidney-shaped. On the inside, they look something like a bee's honeycomb. The organs are made of a number of six-sided columns packed together. Up to a thousand jelly-filled disks are stacked in each column. When an electric ray makes electrical impulses inside its body, electricity builds up inside the disks. Electric rays make enough electricity inside their electric organs to deliver a shock of 8 to 220 volts. Shocks like these will stun or kill fish, and the stronger ones can knock a human unconscious.

Some species of electric rays can direct the shock upward from their backs. Since most rays are usually on the bottom, many attacks come from above. An electric shock is a pretty good defensive weapon against a predator's attack from above—or a person's foot stepping downward!

Some electric rays deliver shocks from the underside of their bodies. These electric rays hide in the sand or mud. When prey swims near, the ray lunges on top of it and zaps the prey with a powerful shock that stuns it. While the confused prey tries to recover, the electric ray has enough time to wrap the prey in its pectoral fins and eat it.

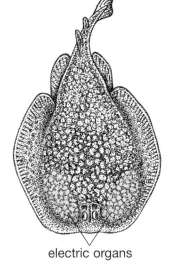

electric organs

Above: *The colored areas on this diagram show where the electric organs are in an Atlantic torpedo, a typical electric ray.*
Left: *An Atlantic torpedo*

33

Some aquariums have tanks large enough to hold rays as big as the southern stingray these people are looking at. Southern stingrays can grow to 7 feet (2 m) wide and 300 pounds (140 kg).

LIFE CYCLE

Because it's so difficult to study rays in the wild, scientists often study captured rays in laboratories. In the past, scientists had trouble keeping large adult rays, and any babies they had, alive in captivity. But now aquariums build and maintain very large tanks. These tanks are healthier for large rays, such as eagle rays, because the rays have more room to swim around. Small skates, like the clearnose skate, live and breed successfully in smaller tanks. Much of our knowledge about mating and birth comes from observation of captive rays.

Rays mate and have young at different ages, depending on their species. Most species of rays have not been studied enough to give a clear idea about the age at which they breed and give birth. Scientists think the ability to mate may also depend on a ray's size—a ray may need to be fully grown before it can mate. Observations of round stingrays that live along the coast of the western United States show that they mate when they are about two-and-a-half years old. Male thornback skates can mate at about seven years of age. But the females are not ready to mate and have young until they are about nine years old.

When blotched fantail rays are ready to mate, many males follow one female.

35

Some rays breed year-round. Others have a **breeding season,** or a certain time of year when they mate. A breeding season is usually timed so the babies will hatch or be born at a time of year when there will be plenty of food available. During the breeding season, a female ray is likely to mate with several males. After mating occurs, females and males do not remain together as pairs.

Often, rays move into shallower water to breed. Females lay their eggs or give birth to their young in shallow waters called nurseries. Sea plants and rocks in shallow waters offer mating rays protection from predators and provide plenty of hiding places and food sources for newborns.

A male Atlantic guitarfish sniffs a female to see if she is giving off a scent that means she is ready to mate.

A close-up of the claspers of a marbled ray

During mating, the male ray uses a tube in his claspers to deposit sperm into the female ray's body. To do this, the male must keep the female close to his body. He holds her by biting into her pectoral fin. Inside the female's body, a sperm joins together with an egg and creates an **embryo**—a baby in the first stages of growth.

The embryos of most rays grow inside their mother's body. A thin shell covers each embryo. Inside the shell, the embryo is attached to a yolk sac that contains food for the embryo. Soon the embryo grows too large for the shell. The yolk sac remains attached to the embryo and continues to nourish it. As the embryo grows, the yolk shrinks. Finally, the yolk can no longer give the embryo enough nutrients. Then the baby receives nourishment from its mother.

The mother's body grows thin strands of tissue that surround each embryo. Some strands enter into the embryo's spiracles. Nutritious material from the mother's body passes through the tissue to the embryo. The nutrients enable the embryo to finish growing.

A southern stingray pup

The embryo needs to grow inside its mother for 2 to 11 months or longer. Then it is ready to be born and survive on its own. A baby ray is called a **pup.** A group of pups born at the same time is called a litter. The number of pups born in a litter ranges from 1 to 15.

Pups may be born headfirst or tail first.

It usually takes only a few minutes for a pup to be born. Stingray pups have a soft covering on their spines, and sawfish pups have a covering on their saw. The coverings protect the mother from being gashed by the spines or saws while the pups are being born. Pups shed the coverings shortly after birth.

Above: *This egg case was released from a winter skate's body just minutes before the photo was taken.*
Right: *A close-up of an egg case with a window opened to show the skate pup inside*

Skates are different from other rays because, like most fishes, they do not give birth to live babies. When a female skate's egg is fertilized and turns into an embryo, a leathery case forms around it. Then the mother skate squeezes the egg case out of her body. The egg case, often called a mermaid's purse, drops to the bottom. A yolk sac inside the case supplies the baby skate with nourishment until it is ready to hatch. It takes 3 to 15 months for a baby skate to hatch, depending on the species. A skate can lay 10 to 200 eggs per year.

A pup's size depends on its species. The disk of an average newborn round stingray is about 3 inches (8 cm) across. It weighs only a few ounces (about 100 grams). Manta pups seem gigantic in comparison. One newborn manta pup's disk was 45 inches (1.1 m) wide. It weighed 28 pounds (13 kg).

Pups are on their own as soon as they are born. After birth, pups begin searching for food. They gobble up small creatures such as shrimp, marine worms, and small crabs and fish.

A newly hatched big skate

Young rays don't eat as much shellfish as older rays. This is probably because their teeth and jaws haven't had time to grow strong enough to crush the shells.

Rays grow more slowly than most other fishes. The pups of larger species, such as manta rays, don't reach their adult size until they are several years old. Smaller rays, such as the round stingray, may be fully grown in about one year. Unless a ray was born in captivity, it's almost impossible to tell how old it is.

A healthy ray can live a long time. Manta rays can live 20 or more years. Freshwater sawfish can live more than 40 years. Most rays have a good chance of living long, healthy lives, because they have few predators. Large sharks, however, particularly hammerheads and great white sharks, eat rays. Human fishers also catch and kill many rays.

This wedgefish is about to be cleaned. Many rays are valued by humans because their fins have a delicious flavor. Some are overfished and becoming hard to find.

RAYS AND PEOPLE

In recent years, certain species of rays have become much harder to find. That means there aren't as many left in the water. Rays are seldom released, even when caught accidentally, because fishers can sell them. People eat rays, especially the pectoral fins. Oil from their livers is used in cosmetics, medicines, and soaps. Sawfish saws are sold for use in the tradional medicines of some countries and as knickknacks in some other countries.

Compared to other fishes, rays have only a small number of young per year. When a large number of rays are caught and killed, it takes a long time for enough babies to be born to replace them. When rays are removed from the water faster than they can be replaced by newborns, scientists say the rays are **overfished.** During the past five years, fishers and scientists have noticed that barndoor, smooth, and thorny skates are becoming very rare. Overfishing is one of the reasons. Some rays have become so rare that they are **endangered.** That means they are in danger of becoming **extinct.** If a species becomes extinct, there are none of that animal left in the world.

Left: *This marbled ray has a rope tied around its tail and part of its tail has been cut off.*
Below: *A beach in Spain littered with trash washed up from the ocean*

The World Conservation Union is an organization that brings endangered animals and plants to people's attention, so that steps can be taken to prevent endangered species from becoming extinct. Several species of sawfishes are currently classified as endangered by the World Conservation Union.

Another threat to rays is that some ray habitats are being destroyed. When people throw trash, such as pieces of metal or old tires, into the water, they litter the clear, sandy bottom. The loose sand a ray uses to partially hide itself is covered. As people build homes and businesses along a coastline, the water nearby is often **polluted** by industrial waste. To pollute the water means to make it dirty by adding harmful materials. For example, oil tankers sometimes leak huge quantities of oil into the ocean. Oil spills have far-reaching effects in the rays' habitat because they kill plants and animals. In many areas, chemicals used as fertilizers in agriculture and on lawns wash into the sea. They often have disastrous effects on the creatures rays eat. Some of these creatures are forced to leave the area. Others die. In either case, since fewer prey animals are available, rays are likely to starve.

There are many things we don't know about rays. Some species have hardly been studied at all. Many questions need to be answered. Do rays communicate with each other? How do they cope with changes to their habitat? Where do rays go when, and if, they migrate?

What's exciting is that many young people are studying to be scientists. They are studying rays and trying to answer these questions. By answering them, they may find solutions to the problems that occur when humans encounter rays. Perhaps they can find ways to work with fishers to reduce the number of rays caught accidentally. Maybe they can develop building plans that won't lead to habitat destruction. The more we all learn, the more likely it is that rays will thrive in the future.

A spotted eagle ray

CLASSIFICATION OF RAYS

All rays currently belong to one large order, the Rajiformes. They are further grouped into smaller suborders.

Scientists have named nine suborders of rays. Features of a ray's body help scientists figure out in which suborder a ray should be placed. Outside body features include the shape of the ray's snout and fins, the location of its dorsal fins, and the kind of tail it has. The shape and structure of a male's claspers are also important. Inside the ray's body, the shapes and sizes of certain bones and the presence or lack of electric organs are some of the features scientists look at.

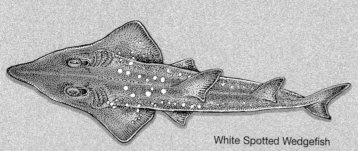

White Spotted Wedgefish

Suborder Rhynchobatoidei (wedgefishes). Angular disk. Small thorns on back. Thick tail. First dorsal fin located over pelvic fins.

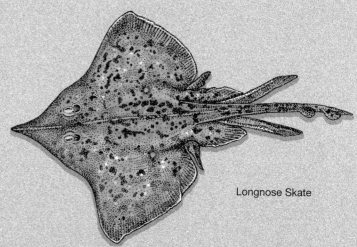

Longnose Skate

Suborder Rajoidei (skates). The only egg-laying rays. Large disk. Slender tail. Tail fin is very small.

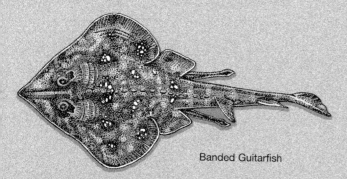

Banded Guitarfish

Suborder Rhinobatoidei (guitarfishes). Angular disk. Small thorns on back. Thick tail. Dorsal fins located far back on the tail.

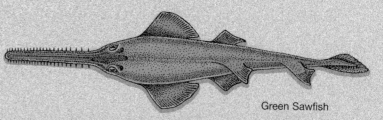

Green Sawfish

Suborder Pristoidei (sawfishes). The only rays with sawlike snouts. Small, triangle-shaped disk. Thick tail.

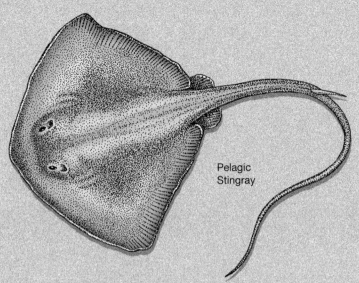

Pelagic
Stingray

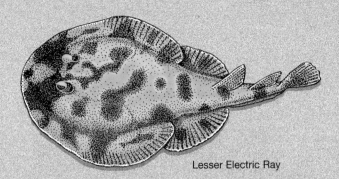

Lesser Electric Ray

Suborder Torpedinoidei (electric rays). Large, round disk. Thick tail. These rays have large electric organs.

Suborder Myliobatoidei (stingrays). Large disk. Slender tail. Stingers on tail. Small tail fin may be present.

Shark Ray

Suborder Rhinoidei (shark rays). Thick, rounded disk at the front of the body. Thick tail. Large thorns on the back. First dorsal fin located over the pelvic fins.

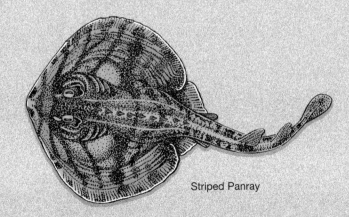

Striped Panray

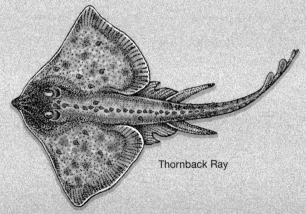

Thornback Ray

Suborder Zanobatoidei (panrays). Large, rounded disk. Large thorns along back. Thick tail. Spots on the body.

Suborder Platyrhinoidei (thornback rays). Large, heart-shaped disk. Large thorns plentiful on back. Thick tail. No spots.

GLOSSARY

adapt: to change the body so an organism can better survive in its environment

ampullae of Lorenzini: a special sensory system for detecting electrical pulses in water

breeding season: a specific time of year when animals mate

carnivore: an animal that eats meat

cartilage: the strong, flexible tissue that makes up a ray's skeleton

clasper: a tubelike organ used in reproduction. Only male rays have claspers.

denticle: a pointed scale that sticks up from a ray's skin

disk: the large, flattened part of a ray's body

embryo: an early stage of an animal that has not yet hatched or been born

endangered: at risk of dying out forever

extinct: when all animals in a species have died out

fossil: the hardened remains of an ancient life-form

gills: organs used in breathing underwater. Gills remove oxygen from water.

habitat: the area where an animal or plant normally lives and breeds

lateral line: a system of pores along a fish's body. It is used to sense the fish's surroundings.

migrate: to move from one place to another during certain times of the year

overfish: to remove too many fish from an area. The remaining fish cannot breed fast enough to replace the fish that have been caught.

pectoral fin: a fanlike fin on the side of a fish used for swimming and steering

pollute: to make water dirty by adding harmful materials

predator: an animal that kills and eats other animals

prey: animals that are eaten by other animals

pup: a baby ray

species: a type of plant or animal

spine: a long, sharp thorn that sticks out from a ray's body

spiracle: a special opening on the top of a ray's body used to suck in oxygen-filled water

thorn: a long, thick, pointed scale

INDEX

ampullae of Lorenzini, 27, 30

birth, 38–39
blotched fantail ray, 35

captivity, rays in, 34
cartilage, 8
claspers, 15, 18, 37
classification of rays, 8, 10, 44–45
cownose ray, 23, 29

diet, 20–22, 28, 39
defenses: electric shock, 33; stinging spine, 7, 11, 18, 31–32, 38
denticles, 16, 22, 31
disk, 10, 18, 25, 32, 39; description of, 13–14

eagle ray, 14, 22, 23, 29, 31, 34; kinds of, 14, 26, 43
eggs, 10, 36, 37, 39
electric ray, 11, 14, 15, 32, 33; atlantic torpedo, 33; coffin ray, 23
embryo, 37–39
endangered, 41–42
eyes, 18, 19, 25

fishers, 40, 41

gills, 18–19; gill slits, 10, 12, 14, 18–19
guitarfish, 12, 15, 17; atlantic guitarfish, 36; giant guitarfish, 41

habitat, 23–25, 42
humans and rays, 6, 31, 34, 40, 41–43

lateral line, 27–28

manta ray, 11, 21, 23, 24, 29; description of, 13, 14; pups, 39, 40
marbled ray, 37, 42
mating, 10, 15, 29, 35–37
migration, 29–30, 43
mouth, 14, 18, 27

panray, 12
pectoral fins, 9, 17, 18, 33, 37, 41; use of, 14, 15, 21, 23
predators of rays, 25, 31, 36, 40

roundray, 29

sawfish, 21, 38, 40, 42; description of, 12, 15, 17; habitat of, 24, 25
senses, 25, 26
shark, 9, 12, 23, 31, 40; whitetip reef shark, 8
shark ray, 12
size, 13, 39
skate, 10, 14, 15, 24, 34, 39; kinds of, 11, 15, 17, 22, 24, 25, 34, 35, 39, 40, 41
skin, 16, 20
snout, 10, 14, 17, 18, 26
spiracles, 18, 19, 37
stingray, 24–25, 31–32, 38, 39; description of, 11, 13, 14, 15; kinds of, 11, 16, 20, 21, 25, 29, 31, 34, 35, 38, 40; *see also* manta ray

tail fins, 15, 18
tails, 9, 11, 15, 16, 17, 31–32
teeth, 10, 22, 40
thornback ray, 12, 14, 17, 27
thorns, 17, 18

wedgefish, 12

young, 29, 36, 38–40, 41

ABOUT THE AUTHOR

Sally M. Walker is the author of many books for young readers, including *Fossil Fish Found Alive: Discovering the Coelacanth* and the early reader *Mary Anning: Fossil Hunter.* "Mermaid's purses" are one of her favorite beachcombing treasures. When she isn't busy writing or doing research for books, Ms. Walker works as a children's literature consultant. She has taught children's literature at Northern Illinois University and given presentations at many reading conferences. She lives in Illinois with her husband and two children.

PHOTO ACKNOWLEDGEMENTS

The photographs in this book appear courtesy of: © Fred Bavendam, front cover, pp. 8 (top and bottom), 41; © David Wrobel/Visuals Unlimited, pp. 2, 19 (bottom), 32 (main), 40; © Doug Perrine/Seapics.com, pp. 4-5, 14 (top), 15, 17 (left), 20, 23, 25 (top), 28 (bottom), 29, 37, 42 (left), 43; © Mark Strickland/Seapics.com, p. 6; © Hal Beral/Visuals Unlimited, pp. 7, 19 (top); © A. Kerstitch/Visuals Unlimited, p. 9; © Ken Lucas/Visuals Unlimited, pp. 10 (left and right), 14 (bottom); © Saul Gonor/Seapics.com, p. 11 (top); © Franco Banfi/Seapics.com, p. 11 (bottom); © Gary Bell/Seapics.com, p. 12; © James D. Watt/Seapics.com, p. 13; © Jeff Jaskolski/Seapics.com, p. 16; © Mark Conlin/Seapics.com, pp. 17 (bottom), 28 (top), 35, 39 (bottom); © Steve Drogin/Seapics.com, p. 21; © Dan Burton/Seapics.com, p. 22; © Michael S. Nolan/Seapics.com, p. 24; © Andrew J. Martinez, pp. 25 (bottom), 33, 39 (top); © Michael Patrick O'Neill/Seapics.com, p. 26; © Phillip Colla/Seapics.com, p. 27; © David Fleetham/Visuals Unlimited, pp. 30, 31; © Marty Sayderman/Visuals Unlimited, p. 32 (inset); © David Kearnes/Seapics.com, p. 34; © Mike Bacon/Seapics.com, p. 36; © John Morrissey/Seapics.com, p. 38; © Ecoscene/CORBIS, p. 42 (right).